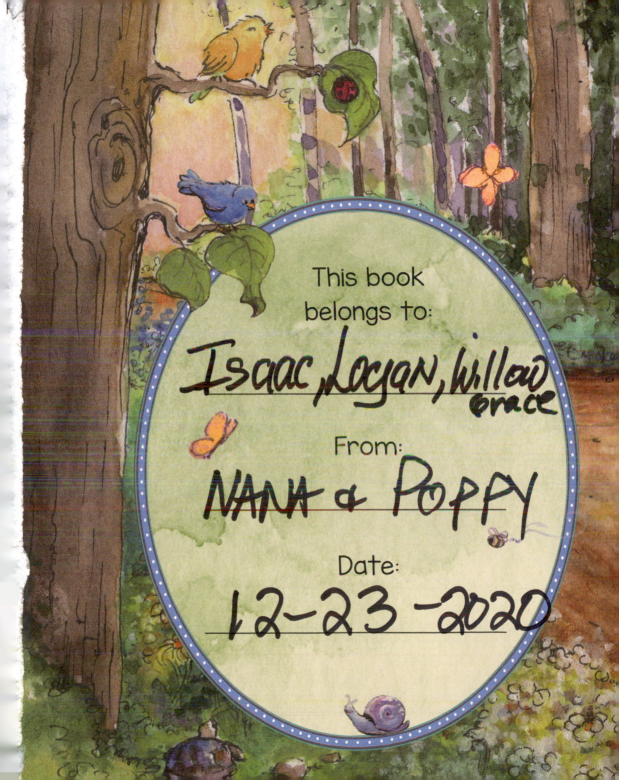

This book
belongs to:

Isaac, Logan, Willow
Grace

From:

NANA & POPPY

Date:

12-23-2020

Copyright © 2019 by Christian Art Kids,
an imprint of Christian Art Publishers,
PO Box 1599, Vereeniging, 1930, RSA

First edition 2019
Illustrations by Marlaine Michie
Images used under license from Shutterstock.com

ISBN 978-1-4321-2965-1

Printed in China

19 20 21 22 23 24 25 26 27 28 – 10 9 8 7 6 5 4 3 2 1

Printed in Shenzhen, China
November 2018
Print Run: 100409

My Own Little
PRAYER BOOK

Dave Strehler

christian
art kids

To my grandson Michael

Children are a gift from the LORD;
they are a reward from Him.

Psalm 127:3

You are God's gift to us!

CONTENTS

Talking to God

When God created the first people Adam and Eve, He enjoyed meeting with them, and they talked to God as a close friend. That is the way God wanted things to be.

But then Adam and Eve disobeyed God and, because of their sin, God could no longer come down to talk with them. And because of sin, no person on earth would be able to see God.

Yet, God still listened to those who wanted to talk to Him. Those who prayed, believed that God would hear them. That kind of faith pleased God.

Some people, however, wanted a god they could see. So they carved idols out of wood and stone and prayed to them.

Guess what happened. Nothing! Because those gods were dead. They had no power at all! But still, the people carried on worshiping statues and people and planets, imagining that these things had the power to help them. But none of them ever did!

Over the years, nothing has changed. Our God is still all-powerful, and idols still have no power.

That is why we pray to the *living* God! And this is how we know that our God is the true God:

- He is the Creator of the universe
- He is the God that the Bible speaks of
- He is the Father of our Lord Jesus Christ
- He is the King of kings.

Because He is God, He hears every prayer we pray and answers each one in the best way.

- God has the **power to answer** our prayers. He created everything there is, so nothing is impossible for Him.
- God **wants to answer** our prayers. He loves us so much that it gives Him pleasure to do things for us.

When we ask Jesus to make our hearts new, we become God's children. That means, we pray to God as our heavenly Father.

And so, when we pray to God, we can call Him *Lord* or we can call Him *Father*, as Jesus did in Matthew 6:9-13 when He taught us to pray:

Our Father in heaven, may Your name be kept holy.
May Your Kingdom come soon.
May Your will be done on earth, as it is in heaven.
Give us today the food we need, and forgive us
our sins, as we have forgiven those who sin
against us. And don't let us yield to temptation,
but rescue us from the evil one.

Amen.

Praising Prayers

We worship God
for who He is
and praise Him
for what He has done.

I Worship You for Who You Are

You are great and powerful, glorious, splendid,
and majestic. Everything in heaven and earth
is Yours, and You are king, supreme ruler over all.

1 Chronicles 29:11

Do you sometimes wonder what God is like? Do you try to imagine what He looks like?

Your thoughts about God may be shaped by what you've heard people say about Him. Perhaps you imagine Him to be like a picture you've seen in a book.

But no one has ever seen God, and that means, no one knows what He looks like. Yet we do know, from what the Bible says, *who* God is and *what* He is like. For example, we know that He is the ruler of the universe, and we know that God has no beginning and no end. We also know that God is everywhere and knows everything. The Bible tells us all that God wants us to know about Himself.

When we worship God we are telling Him what amazes us about Him. We tell Him how wonderful He is!

SOMETHING TO DO:

Instead of trying to imagine God, use a sheet of paper or a paper plate to write words that describe Him. You could decorate it with a few colors and glitter.

Lord God Almighty,
Thank You that You are so awesome. You are the Creator who holds everything together and keeps everything going.
You are in control of the whole world and You are my Lord.

Amen

I Worship You for Your Holiness

Exalt the LORD our God!
Bow low before His feet, for He is holy!

Psalm 99:5

God is holy. That means, God is completely perfect and good.

God's holiness shines brighter than the midday sun. Where God is, all darkness must flee (John 1:4-5).

The Bible compares our sin to darkness, which means that we should be afraid of God and run away because no one can even look at Him and live (1 Timothy 6:16). But because Jesus makes us clean by taking away our sin, we can worship God without fear. In fact, His holiness makes us feel safe and loved. We can trust God completely, for He only does what is good. Because of our faith in Jesus Christ, we can boldly come close to God, and humbly bow down to worship Him.

SOMETHING TO DO:

Go get your hands all dirty,
but don't touch anything!
Then go and wash your hands well.
That's what Jesus does in your heart
when you ask Him to forgive you.
He makes you clean inside so that
you can worship a holy God.

Heavenly Lord,
I worship You for the beauty of
Your holiness. I bow down to You and say,
"Only You are truly holy!" Thank You that You
have shone Your light into my heart and made
me pure.

Amen

I Worship You for Your Great Power

Great is our Lord and mighty in power;
His understanding has no limit.

Psalm 147:5

Power can create and power can destroy. With our hands, we can make things and break things.

But only God has the power to create something from nothing. By His powerful words He created the world and everything that lives. He created the sun, moon and stars.

God is almighty – He has unlimited power, and because of that, He is able to help you. God says, "Don't be discouraged, for I am your God. I will strengthen you and help you. I will hold you up with My victorious right hand" (Isaiah 41:10).

God has the power to help us in any situation, and He also gives us His strength to face any situation.

SOMETHING TO DO:

Reading a psalm helps us to
see many ways to worship God.
Read a short psalm today
(like Psalm 100) and try to
learn a verse from the Psalms.

Mighty God,
When I look at the night sky and see the work
of Your fingers — the moon and the stars You
set in place, I wonder why You would think
about me and care for me. And yet that same
power is now working in me and helps me to do
what pleases You.

Amen

I Worship You for Your Loving Kindness

Because Your love is better than life,
my lips will glorify You.

Psalm 63:3

The Bible tells us that the Lord's love reaches to the heavens. That means, everyone under the heavens is covered and surrounded by His love.

You may wonder how God is able to love so many people, and whether He really loves each one the same. The Bible assures us that "The LORD is good to everyone. He showers compassion on all His creation" (Psalm 145:9).

Even when you've messed up and feel unloved, God's love for you will never change. We know this because while we were sinners, God showed His great love for us by sending Jesus to die for us and take away our sin (Romans 5:8).

And even when you feel small and unnoticed, God – who knows when a little bird falls – gives you an invisible hug.

SOMETHING TO THINK ABOUT:

You can dance, kneel or bow down before
the Lord when you worship Him. You can
sing, clap, lift your hands, or shout for joy
when you praise Him for His great love.
Let your heart tell you how to worship!

Loving Father,
I praise You that You love me with an everlasting
love. Your great love for me will never change, no
matter where I am, how I feel or what I do. The
way You watch over me and care for me makes
me feel very special.

Amen

I Praise You for the Beauty of Nature

O LORD, what a variety of things You have made! In wisdom You have made them all. The earth is full of Your creatures.

Psalm 104:24

No two snowflakes have the same pattern, and no two trees grow exactly the same. No two people are perfectly alike, and that means there's only one person exactly like you. Creation is amazing!

Can you imagine if there were no color and the whole world was a murky grey. Or imagine if everything were flat and had no shape.

All around we see God's awesome creation. "The heavens declare the glory of God, and the sky displays what His hands have made" (Psalm 19:1).

Jesus said that if we – as God's special creation – don't praise Him, even the rocks would cry out! Nature itself would shout out praises to honor the Creator. So let *us* rather praise our God.

SOMETHING TO THINK ABOUT:

See how many different shaped
leaves you can find and tape
them to a sheet of paper.
Or, you could look for different colored
leaves and give each color a special name.

Lord God,
I am amazed every time I see a little ant, or
a colorful butterfly, or a huge elephant. I love
rolling on green grass and climbing trees. You
know the stars by name and count the grains of
sand on the beach. Wow! You are amazing.

Amen

I Praise You
for Giving Me Life

I will give thanks to You because
I have been so amazingly and miraculously made.

Psalm 139:14

If you have watched someone knit, you'll know that it takes time and care. At first, it's hard to guess what is being knitted because there doesn't seem to be a pattern or shape. But when the handiwork is finished, it is beautiful and it has a purpose, just like you!

The psalmist said, "You created every part of me; You knitted me together inside my mother" (Psalm 139:13).

You didn't just happen. God made you the way you are, and that's what makes you perfect. He is the one who made your body and gave you special abilities. You are God's handiwork (Ephesians 2:10)!

SOMETHING TO DO:

Make a poster with your name and age;
a picture of yourself and perhaps a thumbprint.
Describe yourself and write the thing you
enjoy and the things you're good at.
Add your favorite Bible verse.

Dear Father,
I praise You for giving me life and holding me
safely in Your hands. Thank You for taking the
time to make me, and now I am just the way You
want me to be. I so enjoy life here on earth, and I
look forward to spending eternity with You.

Amen

I Praise You
for Your Perfect Plan

"I know the plans that I have for you," declares the LORD.
"They are plans for peace and not disaster,
plans to give you a future filled with hope."

Jeremiah 29:11

Before you were born, God worked on a wonderful plan for your life. In Psalms it says that God planned every single day: "All my days were written in Your book and planned before a single one of them began."

God has even planned when and where people should live (Acts 17:26), and you are part of that plan. He put you in the right family, at the right time, and in the right place.

God also allows the important decisions *you* make to be a part of His plan. And even when things go wrong in your life, God plans for good to come to you through whatever happened.

SOMETHING TO DO:

Ask someone to help you work out how many seconds are in a day. God has planned for every second of your life, and that's a lot of planning!

Dear God,
When I see the moon and stars You set in place, I wonder why – as small as I am – You would think about me and care for me. Your plan for my life makes me feel safe and loved. I praise You for holding together the whole universe and carefully watching over me.

Amen

I Praise You for Keeping Me Close

"I have loved you with an everlasting love;
I have drawn you with unfailing kindness."

Jeremiah 31:3

One of the best things in life is feeling close to someone who loves you; and one of the worst things is feeling lost, unwanted or alone.

The Lord loves you more than you will ever know. He will always keep you close to Himself, just as a shepherd loves and protects his lambs.

Like silly sheep, every one of us has run away and got lost at one time. We were far from God! But God sent Jesus to go find us, save us, and bring us back to Him.

The Lord will never let go of us! He carries us in His arms, holding us close to His heart (Isaiah 40:11).

SOMETHING TO DO:

Draw a shepherd
holding a sheep, and
glue a bit of cotton wool
on to the sheep.
Draw an arrow pointing to the
sheep and write, *That's me!*

Heavenly Lord,
You made my heart want to belong, and I'm
so glad I belong to You. My heart sings for joy
because I believe what You have said in Your Word.
I praise You for holding on to me and saying, "Do
not be afraid. I am here to help you."

Amen

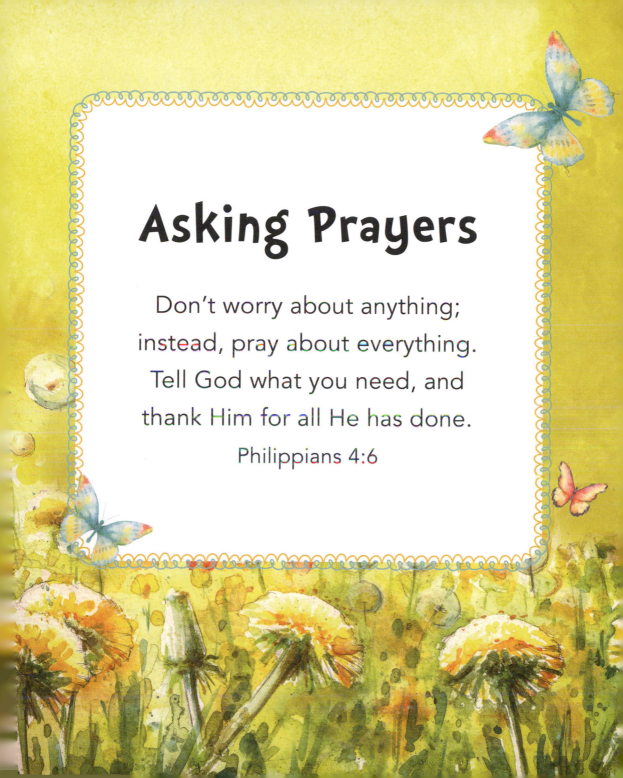

Asking Prayers

Don't worry about anything;
instead, pray about everything.
Tell God what you need, and
thank Him for all He has done.

Philippians 4:6

I Ask You for What I Need

My God will meet all your needs according to
the riches of His glory in Christ Jesus.

Philippians 4:19

When Jesus taught His disciples to pray, He began by worshiping His Father. Then He prayed for His daily needs, like food. Yes, Jesus needed to eat!

While there may be enough food in your home at the moment, and probably some money to buy more, you too should ask God daily to give you what you need.

Asking reminds us that God is the one we depend on for every little thing. Asking is also a way of saying to God that although we are able to do some things, every good and perfect gift actually comes from Him.

As the birds rely on their heavenly Father to feed them, so God wants us to rely on Him (Matthew 6:26).

SOMETHING TO THINK ABOUT:

Think of a way God could use you to help meet a need. Is there someone with whom you could share a bit of what you have?

Dear Father,

When I give thanks before a meal, I am reminded that You made a way for me to have food. When I have clothes to choose from, I remember that You are the One who gives us all things. And so I ask that You will give me whatever I need to get through each day.

Amen

I Ask for Your Protection

For He will order His angels
to protect you wherever you go.

Psalm 91:11

The world is not perfectly safe. You could get hurt on the playground or trip over something at home. You will probably get cut and bruised and scraped as you go through life. Thankfully, your body is able to heal itself as best it can.

Although we do have God's promise of protection, we can pray the power of that promise over our particular situation. That is what Ezra did before he and others set off on a long journey. He prayed that God would protect them, and their children, and all their things (Ezra 8:21).

However, we should not expect God to keep us safe if we take dangerous risks. Jesus told the devil that we should never test God's loving care by being foolish. So be safe! Obey the rules, and trust God.

SOMETHING TO THINK ABOUT:

Can you think of someone in the Bible
who was protected by angels?
(He was thrown into a den of lions.)
His name was ...

Almighty God,
I trust You to look after me and keep me
safe. Please watch over me and protect me
from things that could harm me. Help me
to be careful when I run and dance and play.
And when I'm away from home or traveling,
remind me of Your Word that says, "You care for
those who trust in You."

Amen

I Ask for Help in Temptation

"Pray that you will not give in to temptation."

Luke 22:40

Temptation does not come from God. He cannot and will not tempt anyone to do wrong.

Temptation comes from God's enemy, the devil. Because he cannot fight against God Almighty, he does what he can to try and get *us* away from God.

When we pray that the Lord will not lead us into temptation, we are asking God to lead us away from situations where we could be tempted to do wrong.

We are also asking God to save us from the tempter's power. Temptation can come to us like a test. When Peter's loyalty to Jesus was about to be tested, Jesus prayed for him. Although Peter failed the test, his faith in God did not fail.

SOMETHING TO REMEMBER:

Temptation is not sin. Even Jesus was
tempted. We only sin when we do what we
know is wrong and give in to temptation.
When we do sin, God is faithful;
He will forgive us if we ask Him.

Dear Father,
You know that I love You. But I am often weak
when it comes to doing what is right. Help me to
think of what Your Word says when I am tempted
to do wrong. Please save me from getting into
situations where I may be tempted, and make a
way out for me.

Amen

I Ask for Wisdom

If you need wisdom, ask our generous God,
and He will give it to you.

James 1:5

King Solomon was not born wise, and he did not learn to become wise. Yet he was one of the wisest people who ever lived. Where did Solomon get his wisdom? He asked God.

Having wisdom is not knowing a lot of stuff, or being super clever. It is knowing the best thing to do or say in a tricky situation. When the way ahead is blocked with a problem, wisdom from God always finds the best way forward.

Unfortunately, Solomon didn't use his wisdom to make good choices for himself. He forgot what was important in life and set his heart on things that didn't last. Wisdom from God can only grow in a heart that is humble and wants to help others (James 3:13).

SOMETHING TO THINK ABOUT:

Is your heart ready for God's wisdom?
Here is a checklist: "The wisdom that
comes from above leads us to be pure,
friendly, gentle, sensible, kind, helpful,
genuine, and sincere"
(James 3:17).

Dear God,
You are the One from whom all wisdom comes.
Thank You that You are willing to share Your wisdom
with me, because I could really do with some.
Please give me wisdom to make good choices in
my life and to help others do the right thing.

Amen

I Pray for
All Those in Charge

Pray for kings and others in power, so we may live quiet
and peaceful lives as we worship and honor God.

1 Timothy 2:2

Most of us don't like to be told what to do, and we don't like
rules. Yet this world would be a terrible place if no one was
in charge and if there were no rules.

Imagine if no one checked that our food is safe, and no
one cared in which direction the traffic should flow. Imagine
if no one stopped bad people from hurting others.

God, who is the King of kings, has given us rules to
make life fair and safe for everyone. He has also put certain people in charge of making sure that those and other
rules are obeyed. Our parents, teachers, and leaders all help
to make it possible for God's will to be done on earth as it
is in heaven.

SOMETHING TO THINK ABOUT:

The Bible says that if we disobey those God has put in charge of us, we disobey Him (Romans 13:2).

Dear Lord,
It surely takes a lot of hard work to lead people who don't agree with the rules. Yet You don't want people to simply do as they please. So I ask that You will give those You put in charge of us, the wisdom and courage to lead everyone with fairness.

Amen

I Pray for Those
Who Don't Know You

"So pray to the Lord who is in charge of the harvest;
ask Him to send more workers into His fields."

Matthew 9:38

Before Jesus went back to heaven, He told His followers to spread the news that anyone can be saved from sin and live in heaven forever one day.

Spreading this good news was not an easy task. The disciples of Jesus weren't trained to preach or start a church.

But they had been with Jesus, so all they had to do was tell people what they had seen and heard. And that is how the Good News of Jesus spread.

Prayer became very important to the followers of Jesus. They prayed for each other not to become discouraged. And they prayed for those who didn't believe – that God's power and love would change their hearts.

SOMETHING TO DO:

Ask someone to help you find
a map of the world. Choose one
country every day and pray for
the children there, that they
would learn about Jesus.

Heavenly Lord,
I pray for the leaders and missionaries
that tell others about You. Help them to
know the best way to spread the Good
News, and give them the right words to
speak. May the hearts of those who
hear about You be glad to take in Your
words, so that many will believe in You
and follow You.

Amen

I Pray for My Family

My people will live in safety, quietly at home. They will be at rest.

Isaiah 32:18

When God made people, it was His idea to put us in families where parents could care for their children and lead them in the way they should go.

In our families we can be our ordinary selves. We can even mess up badly and still be loved. In families we learn about life and love; about caring and sharing; about forgiving and accepting.

God gives parents some helpful verses in the Bible about how to bring up their children. He also tells children about their important part in the family, which is to love and respect their parents.

Because parents have so much to take care of, God is pleased when children honor their parents by helping them and praying for them.

SOMETHING TO DO:

How about asking your mom or dad if there
is something you could pray about for them.
If you have a brother or sister, think of
something you could ask God to help them with.

Heavenly Father,
Thank You for the wonderful family You
put me in. I know that we all make mistakes, yet
mistakes help us to stay humble and to forgive.
Help me to be patient and kind to everyone in
the family. Please help my dad and mom to have
enough time and energy to do all the things that
need to be done.

Amen

I Pray for Something Personal

Do what the LORD wants, and He will
give you your heart's desire.

Psalm 37:4

At times, something may be going on in your heart that you
don't really want to talk about. It may be so small that you
wonder whether others would care to listen. It may be so big
that you can't even put it into words.

God has time to listen to what your heart is saying... and
He has the power to change things for you. He cares about
every little thing that is going on in your life. If it matters to
you, it matters to Him.

Your heart may be feeling so heavy that it makes your
shoulders droop. Let Jesus take your heavy
load and give you His peace. Or, perhaps you would like to ask the Lord
for something special. Jesus said
we can ask for anything in prayer
and it will be given to us.

SOMETHING TO DO:

Find a quiet place to pray about
whatever is on your heart.
Write a word or draw a picture to remind
you of your prayer, and keep it safe.

Dear God,
You know how I feel and what I am thinking right
now. From where I am I don't see things the way
You do, but I trust You to take care of what I'm
asking for. Although I'm not sure how or when
You will answer, I know that You will. Thank You
for listening and for being there for me.

Amen

Thanking Prayers

Give thanks to the LORD,
for He is good!
His faithful love
endures forever.

1 Chronicles 16:34

I Thank You for My Health

The L<small>ORD</small> will help them when they are sick
and will restore them to health.

Psalm 41:3

Because Adam brought sin into the world, no person on earth has a perfectly healthy body. If we were perfect, our bodies wouldn't get old, and we would never die!

Besides not being perfect, our bodies are also quite fragile. We all get hurt or become sick at some time. Paul said that our bodies are like a flimsy tent. But our sure hope is that one day we will have new bodies that are perfect and that will last forever (2 Corinthians 5:1).

Even though you may have an allergy, or a part of your body doesn't do what it should, you can still thank God for your health. If you are breathing, you're alive, and that means there is something to be thankful for.

SOMETHING TO DO:

Draw a picture of yourself
with a smiley face, ears, arms, hands,
legs and feet. Every day, thank the
Lord for one part of your body,
and imagine what life would be like
without that part.

Dear God,
Thank You for every morning that I can get out of
bed. Thank You for each day that I feel completely
well. Thank You for all the inside parts of my body
that work together all on their own. Help me to look
after my body because Your Spirit lives in me, and
that makes my body like a beautiful temple.

Amen

I Thank You for My Daily Food

Tell God what you need,
and thank Him for all He has done.

Philippians 4:6

God created everything through the power of Jesus. There is nothing anywhere that has not been made by Him, including all the delicious food in nature.

Yet when Jesus came to live on earth, He thanked God the Father for providing His food.

Even when Jesus turned a few loaves and fish into a meal for five thousand people, He gave thanks to His Father for the food. And when He was invited to stay for a meal in the home of two strangers, He thanked His Father for the bread.

When we sit down to a meal, or buy groceries at a shop, we may easily forget that all these things are a gift from our heavenly Father. We should always remember to stop and thank Him for everything He gives us, just as Jesus did.

SOMETHING TO DO:

Make a poster of your favorite food by cutting pictures from cereal boxes, wrappers, and food adverts. Then glue or tape the pictures on to the cardboard. Use the poster to remind you to be thankful for all the yummy food you eat.

Lord God,
Thank You for my daily food. Thank You for the colors and flavors that make the food taste so good. Your Word says that just as You faithfully feed every little bird, You will also take care of me. May I never get tired of saying, "Thank You," for the smallest thing.

Amen

I Thank You for My Friends

Every time I think of you, I give thanks to my God.

Philippians 1:3

David and Jonathan were best friends. Both were young and brave, and they trusted the Lord.

Jonathan's father was a king, which meant that Jonathan would also have been king one day. But the Lord wanted David, a shepherd, to be the next king.

Because of this, King Saul disliked David and was angry that he and Jonathan were such good friends. Saul even wanted to kill David, but Jonathan helped him escape. This made Saul very angry!

Jonathan even gave David his sword and his belt to show that he was willing to let David be the next king. And so, the two friends brought out the best in each other, stuck together, and were loyal to the end.

SOMETHING TO DO:

Think of three things you like
about your friend. How about telling
your friend why he or she is so special?
Think about what makes you a good friend.

Dear Lord,
I want You to know that You are my best friend.
You really understand me and care about me.
Thank You, too, for all the other friends You have
given me. It's such fun when we play together and
do the things we enjoy. I guess it can't be fun to
be alone and not have anyone to talk to. So help
me to be a friend to someone who needs a friend.

Amen

I Thank You for Answered Prayers

I thank You for answering
my prayer and giving me victory!

Psalm 118:21

God loves rescuing us from trouble and giving us what we need. He wants us to ask Him for help because our trust in Him makes our faith strong. And when He answers, *He* is the One who gets our thankful praise.

One day, ten men who had a bad skin disease called out to Jesus to heal them. Jesus told them to go show themselves to the priests, who would be able to check whether they'd been healed.

On their way, their skin became clean and they knew they were well again. However, while nine of them went on their way, one man went back. When he found Jesus, he fell at His feet and thanked Him.

That is what God wants us to do when He answers our prayers.

SOMETHING TO DO:

Make a list of the things you pray for.
Then patiently watch for God's answer and
keep on praying. When God answers a prayer,
thank Him for what He has done and then
make a tick next to the item.

Lord God,
When You answer my prayers, it is not just a
victory in my life; it is a victory for Your
kingdom. I know that You answer each prayer
in the best way, even if it's not the way I had
hoped or expected. Thank You that You are
faithful to every promise You have made, and
that You have the power to do what You have
promised.

Amen

I Thank You That You Are Good to Me

Give thanks to the LORD Almighty, for the LORD is good;
His love endures forever.

Jeremiah 33:11

A good shepherd loves his sheep. He will do whatever it takes to protect and care for them. David was a shepherd like that. He often thought of God as being our shepherd, and us being the sheep of His pasture.

In Psalm 23, David says that the Lord is our Shepherd because He cares for our needs. He leads us to places where it is safe and peaceful. That is how He gives us new strength on the inside. He guides us along paths that lead to goodness. And even though we walk through a dark valley, we don't need to be afraid because He is right beside us. His guiding hand comforts us, and His Spirit blesses us so much that our hearts overflow with joy.

That is why the Lord is called the Good Shepherd.

SOMETHING TO DO:

Try to learn Psalm 23,
a verse at a time.
Do you think you could do that?

Dear God,

Thank You that You are so good to me! You are so kind and patient and forgiving. You shield me with Your favor and love. David said in Psalm 23 that Your goodness and mercy will always be with me. That means, Your blessing will surround me every day for the rest of my life. And then I will be with You. Lord, You are so good to me!

Amen

I Thank You That We Can Go to Church

I was glad when they said to me,
"Let us go to the house of the LORD."

Psalm 122:1

There is something special about getting together with others who love the Lord.

It pleases our heavenly Father when His family meets to worship Him. Whether it is a kids' group or an all-ages church, we can sing to God, pray for one another, learn about the Bible, and encourage each other. And because each one in the family is different, our time together is all the more exciting.

No family is perfect, and it may surprise you that God's family isn't perfect either. That helps us to be ourselves. We can feel comfortable without pretending to be what we're not; and as ordinary followers of Jesus, thank God for having brought us together.

SOMETHING TO DO:

How about finding two friends to
share with and to pray for. That way,
God connects you to each other
even when you're not together.

Heavenly Father,
Thank You that You have chosen me to belong to
Your family. That means, I have lots of brothers
and sisters as well as older people who care
for me. Thank You that we can get together and
worship You by praying and singing praises. As Your
Word tells me, may I not give up getting together
with those who believe in You.

Amen

I Thank You
That We Have a Bible

All the kings of the earth shall give You thanks,
O Lord, for they have heard the words of Your mouth.

Psalm 138:4

One day, Jesus told a story of a farmer who went out to his field to sow seed.

Some of the seed fell on the footpath, and the birds ate it up. Some fell on rocky ground where the roots of the plants struggled to go down. Other seed fell among weeds that grew up and choked the plants. But some seed fell on good soil where the plants grew strong.

The seed is the Word of God that falls on the hearts of people. Some don't want to hear God's Word. Others forget what they've heard or become distracted. But when we read the Bible and obey it, it is like seed that falls on good soil. God's Word grows in our hearts and becomes a harvest of goodness.

SOMETHING TO DO:

If you have a picture Bible or an ordinary
Bible, treasure it more than any other book!
Read a little every day so that the words
in the Bible find their way to your heart.

Dear God,
I believe that every word in the Bible is from You.
When I read it, it is as if You are speaking those
words to me. Thank You that You have given me
Your promises in writing. Thank You that there
are so many examples in the Bible of how I should
live. May my heart always be ready to take in Your
seeds of truth.

Amen

Thank You That You Are Always with Me

The LORD your God will always be at your side,
and He will never abandon you.

Deuteronomy 31:6

When Noah was in the ark, God was with him. When Joseph was in a pit, God was there. When Daniel was in the lions' den, God was close to him. When Jonah was inside the fish, God heard his prayer.

While we're on earth, we cannot see God, and we may not even feel Him close to us. But Psalm 139 assures us that wherever we go, God is there. If you had to fly up as high as you could, or dig down as deep as you could, or travel as far as you could, God's right hand would still be holding on to you.

God is with us when times are good, even if we forget to think about Him. And He will stay with us when times are bad, just as He stayed with the three men who were thrown into the fiery furnace.

SOMETHING TO THINK ABOUT:

Have you ever run so fast that you left your shadow behind? Of course not, because you can't. It is the same with God. He will always be with you!

Lord God,
I believe that You are with me right now. And even when I do wrong and feel far from You, You are still there to listen to me and love me. Thank You that You promised never to leave me, and thank You that I belong to You forever and ever.

Amen

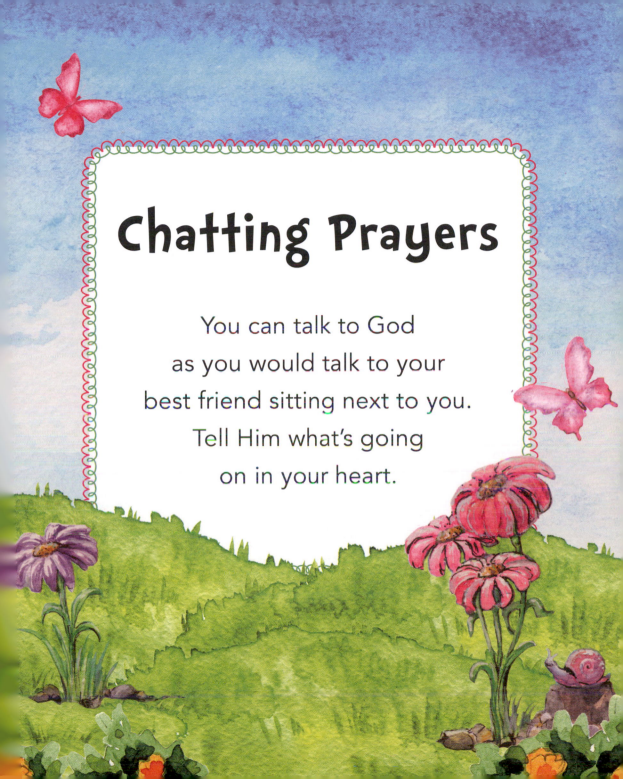

Chatting Prayers

You can talk to God
as you would talk to your
best friend sitting next to you.
Tell Him what's going
on in your heart.

Lord, I Noticed That...

O God, You have taught me from my earliest childhood, and I constantly tell others about the wonderful things You do.

Psalm 71:17

One thing about kids is that they notice things. Being small, kids see things that grown-ups would hardly notice. And because they keep discovering new things, life is filled with exciting adventures.

It could be that you noticed how the petals on a flower fit together, or how a little bug slowly crawls up a blade of grass.

Have you perhaps listened to a well-known Bible story and noticed something new? Or you prayed for someone and saw a change take place?

Maybe you've noticed that a friend at school doesn't seem happy, or that your mom looks worried.

Whenever you notice something, chat to the Lord and tell Him about it because it is important to Him.

SOMETHING TO DO:

Place a bean between two layers of cotton wool and put it in a saucer. Wet the cotton wool and keep it damp. Wait a few days and watch God do a miracle.

Dear Lord,

As I notice things, I try to see how You make everything work together. Even though my faith is like a small seed, may my wonder about You and Your creation make my faith grow like a big tree. What is small to me isn't small to You, Lord, that's why I'm glad You are interested in the little things I tell You.

Amen

Lord, I Want to Be...

For we are God's masterpiece.
He has created us anew in Christ Jesus,
so we can do the good things He
planned for us long ago.

Ephesians 2:10

Have you thought about what you would like to be when you grow up? Maybe you've seen someone doing a certain job, and thought, *I want to be like that!*

Some people like getting a job done, others enjoy being creative, and some love caring for people.

Did you know that before you were born, God worked on a special plan for your life? Then He made you with all you need for that plan to happen.

At the right time God will show you what His plan is. But what He wants for you now, is to be like Jesus.

What you will *do* one day, is something God will show you step by step. In the meantime, keep dreaming about what God has put in your heart.

SOMETHING TO DO:

Make a little pot out of
modeling clay. As you make it,
think of how God is shaping you.

Dear God,
Sometimes when I think about things, I start
dreaming about what I will be when I'm big.
I pray that my dreams of what I want to be
may be shaped by Your plans for me. Whatever
I become, may I always be what You want me
to be: kind, loyal, pure and humble.

Amen

Lord, I Want You to Know...

You know what I am going to say even before I say it, Lᴏʀᴅ.

Psalm 139:4

The Lord loves it when we are honest with Him. We don't need to pretend that we are doing just fine when we are not.

Maybe you're struggling to pray because your thoughts drift off in all kinds of directions. Or perhaps you are trying to be good but then something goes wrong and things end in a mess.

On the night before Jesus was crucified, He and the disciples were in a garden. Jesus asked Peter and two others to pray for Him. But instead of praying, they fell asleep. Oh no!

But when Jesus had risen from the dead, He talked to Peter about love. Peter knew that Jesus could see his heart, and said, "Lord, You know all things. You know that I love You."

SOMETHING TO DO:

Cut a heart out of paper. On it, draw or write whatever is on your heart, for example: *I love Jesus; I am forgiven; Jesus lives here; I sing for joy; Jesus understands my heart.*

Dear Lord,
You know all things. You know what I'm thinking and what I'm going to say. Yet You still like me to tell You what is going on in my heart. And so, I want You to know that I sometimes struggle to do what is right. I also want You to know that I love You and will always try to please You in all that I do.

Amen

Lord, I Want to Tell You...

Fill your minds with those things that are good
and that deserve praise: things that are true,
noble, right, pure, lovely, and honorable.

Philippians 4:8

There are so many things in the world that the Lord has given us to enjoy. What are some of *your* favorite things?

When friends have played with you, do you tell them what fun you had? When your mom or dad spends time with you, do you tell them how special that feels?

Our heavenly Father also wants to know what makes you happy. It could be the sound of rain, or the smell of freshly baked bread, or the warm sunshine on a cold day. Perhaps you feel good when you get tucked into bed at night, or when your dog snuggles up close.

Even small things like licking out a mixing bowl, climbing a tree, or hearing your favorite song, can turn an ordinary day into an extra happy day.

SOMETHING TO DO:

See how many things you can praise
God for. Whenever you see, smell,
taste, feel, or hear something that
makes you happy, tell the Lord about it.

Dear Lord,
I want to tell You how happy I am to feel safe
and loved. I want to tell You that I enjoy listening
to stories. I want to tell You how good it feels to
sit down to a warm meal. Thank You, Lord, that
whenever I fill my mind with good thoughts, I find
that there's no room for bad thoughts.

Amen

Lord, I'm Feeling Sad

He heals the brokenhearted and
bandages their wounds.

Psalm 147:3

Sadness may come suddenly, or slowly, as we miss someone we love or something we treasure.

When one of Jesus' best friends died, He felt a deep sadness for the family, and cried with them. He felt what it is like when a close relationship comes to an end. But Jesus came to give us hope of a new life in heaven where there will be no more pain and no more tears.

Perhaps you, too, are sad today because someone close to you has died. You may be sad for another reason. Perhaps your pet has died or run away. Or maybe you are moving to a far-away place.

The Lord says that He counts your tears and stores them up (Psalm 56:8). In other words, He will not forget your sadness and He will give you new hope.

SOMETHING TO DO:

What is one of the happiest or
funniest memories you have?
Draw a picture of that special time.

Dear Jesus,
I am so sad right now. You know what my heart
feels like because You came to earth to be like
us. That is why You share my sadness, and with
Your love You comfort me. Each of my tears
is precious to You because it comes from my
tender heart. I pray that I may feel Your loving
arms hold me close and that my sadness won't
last too long.

Amen

Lord, Sometimes
I Feel Afraid

When I am afraid, I put my trust in You.

Psalm 56:3

Has anyone said to you, "Don't worry – don't be afraid"? That is what God said to Joshua, Gideon and other mighty men. That is what Jesus said to the disciples.

Fear can make you feel alone and helpless. You may be thinking, *it's only "little me" facing this big scary thing*. That's when it is time to turn your fear to faith. All you need to do is trust God. He has promised to help you and protect you.

But remember, not all fear is bad. Being afraid is okay if it keeps you from doing something dangerous. However, if there is someone who makes you feel afraid, you should tell your mom or your teacher about it. And if you feel afraid but you don't know why, ask God to give you His peace.

SOMETHING TO DO:

Give your fear a nickname and write
it on a piece of paper. Cut the shape
of a cross from another piece of paper,
and glue the cross over your fear.

Heavenly Father,
You know that I am afraid sometimes. It is not
that I don't trust You to look after me. It is just
that I imagine something bad may happen and I
become afraid. I feel so small and helpless when
I'm afraid; that's why I need You. You are big and
powerful and caring. Mighty God, I now trust You
to protect me and keep me from harm.

Amen

Lord, I Feel Angry

Don't let evil conquer you,
but conquer evil by doing good.

Romans 12:21

What has made you angry? Did someone hurt you? Did someone disappoint you? Were you teased? Were you treated unfairly?

Perhaps you got upset as you struggled with a task. Or maybe you felt frustrated because things didn't work out the way you wanted them to.

The wrong way to deal with anger is to shout, destroy things or hurt someone. Doing that is never helpful and only makes one angrier. The right way to tame anger is by talking about it, forgiving, and by doing something good to distract those angry thoughts.

Your heart cannot store anger as well as joy. So don't let anger steal the place of your joy!

SOMETHING TO THINK ABOUT:

If something or someone made you angry,
how would you like things to work out?
Maybe there's something you can do,
or maybe you just need to keep
praying for God to change things.

Dear God,
You know what has upset me. I should just forget about it, but I can't. The feeling just doesn't go away! So I want to ask You to fill my heart with Your peace and joy. Help me to remember that no one is perfect. Help my heart to become calm as I think of Your gentle, caring smile. Thank You for understanding how I feel.

Amen

Lord, I Feel Pushed Away

Turn to me, LORD, and be merciful to me,
because I am lonely and weak.

Psalm 25:16

We all want to feel special to someone. Your heart needs love just as your body needs food. When others don't want to spend time with you, your heart feels empty and lonely.

Hagar, a servant, was chased away from the family she'd been working for. She wandered off with no one to care for her. But God saw her sitting in the desert, crying. So the Lord Himself took care of her and encouraged her.

There was a leper who had no friends. No one came near him because of his terrible skin disease. But Jesus went up to him. He put his hand on the man so that he could feel the touch of a caring friend.

In the same way, the Lord cares for each one who is lonely and feels pushed away.

SOMETHING TO DO:

Be courageous and go find someone
else who is lonely. Soon you'll have
a loyal friend to talk to and play with.

Dear Lord Jesus,
Thank You that You chose me to be Your friend.
That means, I have at least one friend who will
always be on my side. But Lord, I would also like
to have a friend to play with because I get bored
and it's no fun. On my own I feel weak, but if
there were two of us, we could help each other.
So I pray, Lord, that You will give me a good friend.
Amen

Urgent Prayers

"Help!"
is the shortest prayer
you can pray when there's
no time to pray long prayers.

Lord, Help!
I'm in Trouble!

"Call on Me when you are in trouble, and
I will rescue you, and you will give Me glory."

Psalm 50:15

Trouble often comes our way when we least expect it. When something bad happens and we don't have a plan, we start to panic. That is what happened with the Israelites.

They had left Egypt where they had been slaves. The king of Egypt sent his army after them to bring them back. But the people could not run away. With mountains on one side and the sea in front of them they were trapped. "Help!" they called out. Then God opened up the sea and made a path for them right through the sea.

The disciples were in a boat. Jesus was with them but He had fallen asleep. A bad storm came up and the boat was about to sink. "Help!" they called. And Jesus got up and calmed the storm.

SOMETHING TO REMEMBER:

It is good to know an emergency number.
When there's an emergency, stay calm!
Call on God, and your prayer will go
straight through to Him.

Lord God,
Sometimes I get into trouble and it feels like
there's no way out. But You are the one who make
a way where there is no way. Sometimes it feels
like the storm is all around me and I'm in a small
boat on the rough sea. But You are with me in the
boat, and You have the power to calm the storm.
So, please help me, Lord!

Amen

Lord, Help!
I'm Lost!

"For I am the LORD your God who takes hold of your
right hand and says to you, Do not fear; I will help you."

Isaiah 41:13

It feels terrible to be lost. We don't know where to go, and
we are afraid that no one will come and find us.

The Bible tells a story of a little sheep that got lost. Maybe
he had wandered away from the others and no one had
noticed. At first, even the little sheep didn't know he was lost
because the shepherd was always around.

But this time, when the shepherd went home with his
flock of sheep, one got left behind. Once they got back,
the shepherd realized that there were only 99 sheep. One
was missing!

So the shepherd went back to look for the sheep. When
he found it, he put the sheep on his shoulders and carried it
back home.

SOMETHING TO REMEMBER:

If you get lost, it's usually best to stay where you are. Know the name and surname of the person you are with (not just "Mommy" or "Uncle Bill").

Dear Lord,
You are my shepherd and You watch over me. That is why You always know where I am. If I ever get lost, help me to be calm and know that You are guiding someone to me. I trust You to keep me safe when I'm in a crowd or all alone, because You will stay with me all the time.

Amen

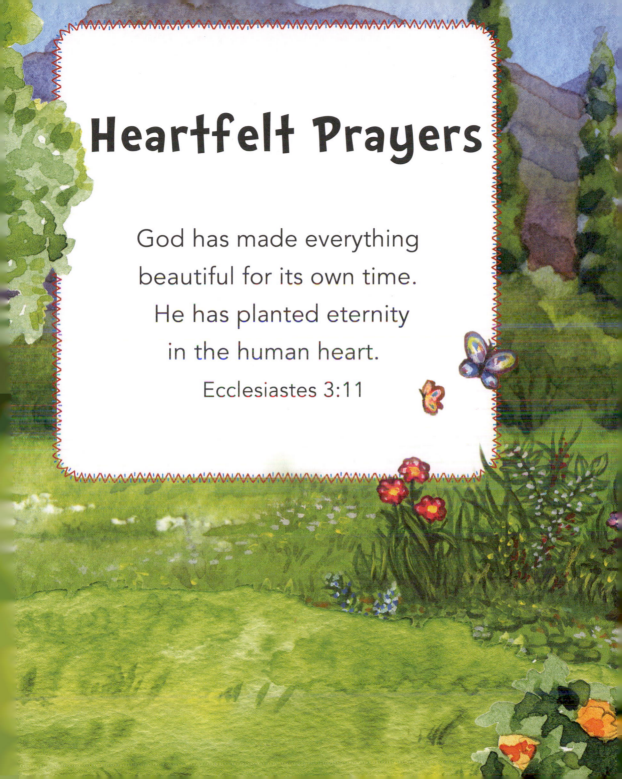

Heartfelt Prayers

God has made everything
beautiful for its own time.
He has planted eternity
in the human heart.

Ecclesiastes 3:11

Lord, Forgive Me

Forgive us our sins, for we forgive
everyone who does us wrong.

Luke 11:4

The heart that we read about in the Bible is a part of us that we cannot see or feel. It is where our good and bad thoughts come from. If we allow bad thoughts to grow in our hearts, we end up doing wrong things.

The wrong we do is called sin, and sin stays in our hearts and makes us feel guilty. There is nothing *we* can do to take our sin away and make our hearts good.

But Jesus wants our hearts to be clean so that we can live beautiful lives for Him. That is why He came to earth. He died on the cross and was buried with our sin. Then God raised Him back to life.

If you want your heart to be clean, all you need to do is ask Jesus to forgive you. He will take away every sin, and never remember it again.

SOMETHING TO REMEMBER:

Your heart is like a storeroom. If you store up
good things in your heart, your attitude will be good
and you'll be less likely to do wrong (Luke 6:45).

Dear Lord,
You know that I try to be good, but I often end
up doing things that are wrong. But I want to
have a clean heart that pleases You, so I ask You
to forgive my sin. In the same way, Lord, I want to
forgive anyone who has been mean to me.

Thank You, Lord, that my heart is clean now. It
is as white as wool!

Amen

Lord, I Belong to You

If you confess that Jesus is Lord and believe
that God raised Him from death, you will be saved.

Romans 10:9

Nicodemus was a good man who believed in God. But Nicodemus knew that *his* life was not like the new kind of life Jesus spoke about.

So Nicodemus went to find Jesus and talk to Him about really knowing God. Jesus saw his heart and said to him, "No one can see God's kingdom unless he is born again."

Jesus was saying that the only way to be part of God's eternal kingdom is to be born into His family. And that can only happen by faith. We can only become a child of God when we believe that Jesus died for our sin and that He makes us truly good.

When we believe, God gives us a new heart where His Spirit can live, and the Holy Spirit is a sign that we belong to Him.

SOMETHING TO REMEMBER:

Even when you don't feel God close to you,
you are still His child. God wants you to
trust Him by believing what He promised.

Dear Lord Jesus,
I believe that You are the only way to God. You
died in my place on the cross so that I can live
forever. I pray that You will forgive me and make
my heart new. I love You! I thank You that I am
Your child and that I will live with You in heaven
forever and ever.

Amen

Lord, Bless Me

Take delight in the L<small>ORD</small>, and He will give
you the desires of your heart.

Psalm 37:4

"Lord, bless me," might sound like a selfish prayer to pray, but that's what Jabez prayed.

He prayed, "Oh, that You would bless me and expand my territory! Please be with me in all that I do, and keep me from all trouble and pain!" (1 Chronicles 4:10).

And God did what Jabez had asked.

The Lord wants to bless us because He loves us. Just as you would ask your mom or dad for something, you can ask your heavenly Father to do something for you. In fact, the Bible says that we don't have because we don't ask God (James 4:2).

To ask for God's blessing is to ask the Lord for the very best of the plans He has for us. If we ask God for something that pleases Him, He will give it to us (1 John 5:14-15).

SOMETHING TO THINK ABOUT:

Psalm 1:3 says a blessed person is like a tree.
Even though seasons (and things)
will change, a blessed person stays
strong and green and fruitful.

Dear Lord,
You already know what I want. But I'd like to ask
You for this so that I will know that the answer
has come from You. I want my faith to grow by
asking this, and I want others to see that I serve
You. If this is also what You want for me, Lord,
please answer my prayer. And as You bless me,
may Your name be made great through my life.

                                        Amen

My Own Prayer

Never give up praying.
And when you pray, keep alert and be thankful.

Colossians 4:2

God would love you to pray your own prayer in your own words. It doesn't matter if your prayer doesn't come out the way you want it to; it is perfect and beautiful to God. He knows what's in your heart, and the Holy Spirit fills in all the words we don't have (Romans 8:26). Your prayer can be as long as you like or as short as you like – just enjoy talking to God.

On the opposite page, you can write your own prayer. (You may want to use a pencil, or perhaps write your prayer on a scrap piece of paper first.)

My Prayer

_____

_____

_____

_____

_____

_____

_____

_____

_____

About Prayer

Yes, no, wait!

Does God answer all our prayers? Yes! That is what He promised to do. Does God answer the way we expect? Not always.

God's ways are better than our ways and His plans are greater than our plans. If we pray for what God wants, He will give us what we ask for (1 John 5:14).

If we pray for something that's not good for us, or if we are being selfish, His answer will be no (James 4:3). God will only give us what we really need.

Sometimes God wants us to wait. His time for doing things is always perfect because He can see how everything will fit together in the best way.

Ask by Faith!

God wants you to ask by faith, believing that He has the power to do what you have asked. He is pleased when you keep on trusting Him even when you cannot see anything happening (Hebrews 11:1).

Keep Asking!

Jesus told a story of a man who knocked on his friend's door in the middle of the night to ask him a favor. At first, the friend didn't want to help him; but because the man carried on knocking, the friend finally got up and helped him.

In the same way, you should knock (and keep knocking), and the door will be opened (Luke 11:9). Ask and keep asking, and God will answer!